What I Did to Make Money on Fiverr From Day One

Diana Loera

The content of this book is copyrighted and owned by Diana Loera/Loera Publishing LLC.

Under NO circumstances is anyone allowed to copy, distribute, resale, modify or use this content as their own.

Anyone who does so, will be fed to my tiger of an attorney.

Thank you for being respectful of others and of copyright law.

Sincerely,

Diana Loera

December 8th   2013

A portion of my sales profit yearly goes to the Independent Cat Society in Westville Indiana.

The Independent Cat Society has been operating on a shoe string budget since the 1970s and work tirelessly to aid cats.

Please neuter your pets and if you want to add a pet to your family- be sure to check out the rescue groups and shelters in your area.

Other Books by Diana Loera/Loera Publishing LLC

Summertime Sangria

Party Time Chicken Wings Favorite Recipes & Bonus Dip Recipes

Awesome Thanksgiving Leftovers Revive Guide

What I Did to Sell More Kindle Books on Amazon

Fifty Years in Chains

Fast Start Guide to Flea Market Selling

Stop Hot Flashes Now

Per Inquiry Secrets Revealed

14 Extra Special Winter Holidays Fondue Recipes

USA Based Wholesale Directory 2013 Edition

What is the Paleo Diet? & Paleo Diet Recipe Sampler

What I Did to Make Money on Fiverr From Day One

www.LoeraPublishingLLC.com

Please visit my blog www.DianaLoera.com and sign up for my email list.

You'll see a sign up box on the left side of my blog.

One of the reasons behind my blog is to be able to share updates, valuable freelance contacts etc. via the blog and via email.

You won't be bombarded with emails as I'm simply way too busy and being a pest just isn't something that I want to be.

You will however, be the first to know when I find things that help me market better such as new freelancers, new services, new products I've found and used to increase my income even more etc.

I want to share ideas and marketing tools with fellow authors and freelancers as much as possible.

I'll also be interviewing authors and freelancers on my blog and you may be one of them if you are on my email list and respond to my request for an interview.

If after reading this book, you have questions about launching your own revenue stream via Fiverr, you're welcome to email me for my input.

Later in this book I'll provide my contact information and also links to Fiverr freelancers that I've used for my own personal marketing.

I hope that you find something helpful in this book.

I wrote it as I started making sales on Fiverr immediately and then discovered many people wait months to get just one sale.

It is my hope that the information I'll be sharing with you helps you make money on Fiverr too.

I do not have any affiliate links in this book nor do I endorse anyone specifically in this book.

The Fiverr gig examples I have included were randomly chosen to provide good examples for those reading this book.

As Fiverr sellers come and go, some of the sellers' links that I listed may expire if the seller quits on Fiverr.

"It takes half your life before you discover life is a do-it-yourself project." - Napoleon Hill

Note from Diana

If you're already on Fiverr and doing well with your revenue stream, this book probably isn't for you.

If you are on Fiverr but not seeing sales – ideally you'll find some tips to help you advance up the Fiverr ranks.

If you've heard about Fiverr but haven't set up an account yet – this book will give you some insight from someone who is making money with Fiverr.

If you have zero clue what on earth Fiverr is but you need to generate income- Fiverr may or may not be for you.

I'm not rolling in Fiverr cashola (yet) but I am seeing a nice steady income and it is increasing.

I wrote this book to help others increase their income on Fiverr and also to determine if Fiverr may be a good revenue generator for them.

Later in this book I'll provide my contact information – If you'd like to contact me, I'll take a look at one of your gigs and see if I can offer any suggestions to help you improve traffic and ultimately sales.

If you have a Fiverr gig that is cool or different or a great service – you're welcome to contact me as it may be one that I will discuss on my blog.

If you've had success (such as by adding a video) and want to share your success story, I'd enjoy having the details for my blog (plus it is free promo for you).

Thank you for buying my book.   I hope you enjoy reading it as much as I've enjoyed writing it.

I welcome verified reviews if you have a few minutes time after you finish the book – I'd appreciate your feedback.

Thank you.

Sincerely,

Diana

Table of Contents

I joined Fiverr as a freelancer as part of my ongoing "experiment" regarding how people can make money in a down economy.

You may have read one of my other books – Fast Start Guide to Flea Market Selling or What I Did to Sell More Kindle Books on Amazon. I've also published a selection of recipe and other non -fiction books.

I've found that there are ways to make money even in a cruddy economy– you just need to know how to find the opportunities.

In some cases, you can work from home, make your own hours and see a decent stream of money come in.

When I wrote Fast Start Guide to Flea Market Selling I did so because my husband and I opened a booth at a local flea market and found why some sellers have been there almost 20 years. Flea market selling can be a profitable gig. I think there are many ways people can make additional income- the challenge is finding out what options are available.

I first came across Fiverr while marketing one of my books and in What I Did to Sell More Kindle Books on Amazon I discussed Fiverr from a buyer's perspective.

Then I started looking at the idea of Fiverr from a seller's viewpoint with one additional benefit – using my years of marketing expertise to increase sales potential.

I started making sales from Day One and found out later that unfortunately this often isn't the case for most people.

When I started looking at random gigs that had zero sales and the seller had been on Fiverr for a few months, I started seeing things that maybe if changed – would help them sell.

I also knew from my own experience what to do to help bring traffic and sales.

I'm not making a HUGE boatload of money on Fiverr – but it is a very nice extra amount of cash every month. It pays some bills and now only a short time after starting on Fiverr- I am seeing a steady amount of sales. Enough to surprise family and friends when I tell them how much I'm making on Fiverr.

I also use Fiverr as a buyer and can, if I choose, apply the money I've earned to buy services and items from other sellers.

We'll discuss what Fiverr is and how it works just in case you aren't very familiar with it but for the most part, I'll be cutting to the chase and giving you feedback regarding what worked – and didn't work for me.

My husband is often floored when he sees my Fiverr revenue. He still can't believe for a little bit of time, I can quickly generate a nice flow of extra revenue.

Sometimes, actually most evenings right after we have supper, I'll log in to my Fiverr account and quickly do a few gigs.

I'll then look at Buyer Requests and most evenings, send an offer in for at least one Buyer Request.

As I am self -employed, I check Fiverr numerous times every day.

The above process is done several times each day but my husband usually only sees the evening Fiverr time when I help several buyers and add $4, $12, $24 or whatever the amount to the family coffers in less than thirty minutes.

This morning, while I enjoyed my first cup of coffee, I completed three orders that came in last night.

This is pretty much a typical day for me.

Of course, this is about my results. You're results may not be the same. I hope they are even better.

I'm not including my Fiverr profile in this book as the last thing I want is for readers to think that this book is a promotion to get more traffic and business on Fiverr.

Later in this book I'll give you my contact info. If you start selling on Fiverr and want to brainstorm a bit about possible gigs, you're more than welcome to contact me.

I've written this book as I Did What I Did to Sell More Kindle Books on Amazon, as if you and I are having a conversation. I'll give you some examples and share my experiences.

I hope my book gives you some insight regarding a possible revenue stream. With our economy being a rollercoaster ride, many people are looking for any way possible to add a little income.

The largest challenges are – gas money, clothes for work, commuting costs (besides gas), daycare costs if needed and having a job that allows you to work when you can especially if you already have a full time job.

Plus, in my opinion, employers are often wanting a lot more work done for less pay.

I could give you several examples but if you or a loved one are working a 9 to 5 job I think you probably know exactly what I mean.

If you can find a way to add to your monthly income from home so you don't need to look for a second job – well, I think that could be beneficial.

The other nice thing about doing Fiverr freelance work is with many gigs you can work remotely on your computer while on vacation. You can work around your kids schedules.

You also set your own schedule. The benefits are many and in most cases the outlay financially to get started on Fiverr is zero.

Last but not least, if you're thinking about starting a freelance proofreading, translation or whatever type of business, Fiverr offers you the opportunity to test the waters. You can see how people respond (or don't respond) to your ideas.

You also will see any potential challenges or questions that crop up.

With this being said, you can test your business idea as a Fiverr gig and see how sound the idea is.

I've read a few other books about selling on Fiverr. While I found them interesting, the common theme was outsourcing your work to others.

I think this would work but that is not the path I've chosen.

This book was written to provide you with an overview of how you can make money on Fiverr and also to jumpstart your brain a bit regarding things you can do via Fiverr to make money.

My Background

I have a background in direct response (infomercial) marketing. I've written hundreds of infomercial scripts and bought millions of dollars in advertising. I've also traveled as a marketing consultant for numerous companies both private and publicly traded.

I've always enjoyed writing and a little over a year ago decided to write and publish a book as self- publishing has become so incredibly easy.

Self –publishing one book quickly turned into self- publishing several books. I read over and over about authors who were self- publishing but weren't seeing any sales.

It didn't take long until I realized that my marketing background was the key in my book success as I was applying the same income generating steps to my books that I did to clients' infomercials.

I was able to cut back on my consulting projects and focus more on my book writing endeavors.

Shortly after realizing the key to my success, I wrote and self-published What I Did to Sell More Kindle Books on Amazon. I am working on volume 2 now and it should be released in early 2014 if not before.

When I was looking for marketing sources for my books I came across Fiverr. I was a bit skeptical regarding the idea of finding someone to handle certain projects such as making book trailers, You Tube banners, do promoting via Twitter and Facebook etc. and only pay them $5.

I quickly found out how to separate the "real deals" on Fiverr from the amateurs and thus was able to freelance out a lot of my marketing projects for as little as $5.

I keep stats (statistics) as I've found over the years it is a powerful business management tool. So I kept stats on the success from the freelancers I hired on Fiverr.

After a while curiosity got the best of me and I thought I would sign up as a freelancer myself on Fiverr and see what type of income I could generate.

We'll talk more about what kind of freelance services you can offer to clients later in this book.

I will say now, even if you can barely type or because you have no real computer knowledge, there are a ton of things you can offer on Fiverr and get paid to do. So please keep reading!

Fiverr – What is It?

Fiverr is a community of freelancers online who offer their services.   The service is called a gig.

This is the site www.Fiverr.com

Gigs range from SEO (search engine optimization) to proof reading to puppet show videos (you read that right), to making origami animals to about anything you can dream of.

Fiverr has rapidly grown the past couple years.

The freelancer is paid $5 via the website. Fiverr keeps $1 of every $5 you earn.

Now if you are like me, and probably like most people, you instantly are thinking What???? $4 bucks???

Here is the beauty of this though – these little projects often take one or two minutes (or less) and can quickly add up.

So if you are making $4 for 2 minutes work……..Now you may have a different outlook on this opportunity.

There are people making a living with just Fiverr gigs and now that I've gotten a taste of the Fiverr juice – I can see why this is occurring.

Like with any opportunity – there are great times to get involved and in most cases it is when something is at the ground level.

Fiverr is still fairly new which is good.

Buyers are coming in more frequently as word gets out about the site.

If you are even remotely considering the idea of becoming a Fiverr seller- now is the time.

If you are looking for an extra revenue stream, this may be a great fit for you.

I'm not going to take up your time to go through setting up an account on Fiverr as I think that entire process is extremely simple.

We'll be discussing the money making part of Fiverr and what I've done to make money. We'll also discuss marketing as I firmly believe my marketing background helped me move into generating sales much faster than someone who doesn't have marketing expertise.

Please keep in mind – Fiverr is, in my opinion, a really easy way to generate income.

You will need to determine if it is a good fit for you or not.

The beauty of Fiverr is that people from all walks of life and with all skill levels can participate.

Yes SEO (search engine optimization) pros have a good chance of generating income but so do people who do origami, paint, write names in the sand on the beach and other things.

You'll see- the possibilities are truly endless when it comes to Fiverr.

Status Levels

Fiverr has several Levels and each level allows you to have more options as far as selling prices etc.

Don't be daunted by the requirements. I reached Level One well before the 30 days. When I first started though I really didn't see it happening but once I started applying marketing techniques – I went to Level One and then on to Level Two quite fast.

Below is what Fiverr currently has posted regarding achieving the levels.

Level One

You've been active on the site for 30 days and completed at least 10 orders while maintaining excellent ratings and a great track record. You'll automatically be promoted to Level One. At this Level, you'll gain additional features making it easier for you to offer more advanced services and generate higher income.

Level Two

You made over 50 orders in the past two months while maintaining excellent ratings and a solid track record. You'll automatically be promoted to Level Two; unlocking advanced sales tools to further expand your services and increase your sales. You'll also receive priority support.

Top Rated Sellers

Top Rated Sellers are manually chosen by Fiverr editors. Promotion is based on the following criteria: Seniority, volume of sales, extremely high rating, exceptional customer care, and community leadership. As a Top Rated Seller, you'll gain access to more extensive sales tools, early access to beta features, and receive VIP support.

Note from Diana – You'll see under Top Rated Sellers, the comment regarding "community leadership" this relates to being active in the Fiverr Forum and helping others.

I haven't starting offering advice in the Fiverr forum. It may be something that I decide to do in the future but as of now I'm pleased to be at Level two and my focus is to keep testing and measuring what works to increase revenue while delivering a great product to those who order my gigs.

Overall - You need to make sure you meet the deadlines, deliver well and receive good reviews.

The first two (meet the deadlines and deliver well) are ones that you have control of as long as the buyer replies in a timely manner with any info that you need. If they don't you can request a mutual cancel based on them not providing what is needed.

As far as reviews – you will get reviews from people and while many are prompt, some are slower to rate you and some simply do not. Don't get all worked up if you have 9 reviews and need that wonderful #10 review to become Level One.

Instead just focus on how to increase your sales. We'll be discussing ways to do so in this book.

Choosing What Gig(s) You Want to Offer

Think about your skills and also think about what you like doing.

So for example – you are great at proofreading. Type "proofreading" in on Fiverr and see who your competition is.

Now here's where it gets a little fun – Do you love being on Facebook?

Type in "Likes on Facebook" – yep, people will pay you $5 (and up) to like things on Facebook. You read that right.

Do you have a Linked In, Twitter or Facebook account?

How about Pinterest?

Your social media site could me a money maker site for you.

People will also pay you to draw, to make signs, to write their name on the beach – yes, that's another great one.

If you live near a beach – people will pay you to write their names, or other message, in the sand and take a photo of it. Is your mind racing yet?

If you are familiar with SEO, various software and anything related to computers - you have a ton of opportunities to make money on Fiverr.

Do you speak a second language? Interested in translating?

The possibilities are truly endless.

We'll talk more about possible gigs as we progress through this book.

Feel free to jot down possible gigs to offer and do so with the understanding that your gigs may totally morph into something else either before; during or after you start getting people contacting you.

The main thing is to jot down a few things that may be possibly Fiverr gigs.

What do you like to do? What tasks are you good at doing?

Okay- you aren't an SEO expert, you can barely type and you don't have a Twitter account with thousands of followers – can you still make money on Fiverr?

I think you have more opportunity on Fiverr than you ever dreamed possible.

Let's stretch our thinking to waaaaay outside the box by looking at some, should we say, interesting? gigs.

Before we begin – you'll note that I calculate $4 a gig.   Fiverr pays $5 per gig but keeps a $1 thus paying you $4. That is why we calculate earnings using $4.

Here are some different gigs to jumpstart your creativity –

Write a name with alphabet soup

http://fiverr.com/anamorris/write-your-text-with-alphabet-soup

Here are other gigs from the same seller- talk about being creative!

http://fiverr.com/anamorris

This one (below) the above seller did for Halloween. She currently has 23 votes – which based on my experience, she probably had even more orders – but 23 actually rated her service.

So 23 orders multiplied by $4= $92 for doing something fairly simple- but her presentation really is impressive. I'm writing this book in December and see she now has added gigs with a Christmas holiday them too.

http://fiverr.com/anamorris/write-anything-on-blackboard-with-halloween-pumpkin

This is a gig for an actual product. He is making a wood wine bottle holder. He currently has 99 review votes so he is definitely doing well.

This is a great example of someone probably making more than $4 per gig completion as he offers upsells so the product can be customized for an additional cost.

http://fiverr.com/jetfumes/make-a-personal-wine-bottle-holder-that-will-be-one-of-a-kind-personalized-gift

This seller will write a message on her body. Before you laugh – 318 votes thus far.

318 x $4=$1272 is in her bank account……..no investment other than whatever she is using to write and then whatever she is using to take the photo.

http://fiverr.com/chicakak/write-and-draw-everything-on-my-face-or-belly

401 orders for this guy from the U.K. who will overreact-

http://fiverr.com/adamrussell/over-react-to-anything-you-want-in-hd

This gig is also listed again further in this book for the great image.   This is a perfect example of thinking outside the box regarding what you can sell.

http://fiverr.com/radishcat/crochet-a-beard-for-you

I thought the above one was a little crazy but then I read all the rave reviews.

Time Frame to Deliver

Fiverr allows you to choose the time frame in which you will deliver be in one day, two days, six days or more.

Speaking from my experience and also from my research, allow yourself time – especially in the beginning but don't make the time frame too long.

Later, after you've had some practice you may want to add a rush option whereas for an extra $5, $10 or other amount you will deliver the order faster.

I have a decent amount of rush orders but most are regular delivery. Rush allows you to make a bit more income which adds up nicely so I'm always glad to see a rush order come in.

 The one thing to remember is – if you add rush – you must check daily as often orders come in on the weekend.

If you are going to be on vacation – you can suspend your gigs or if you're like me and have gigs you can do from anywhere – I just take my laptop with and carry on with business as usual.

Keywords

Keywords are an important part in being found.

Type in keywords on the Fiverr site that you are thinking about using and see what comes up.

Don't be afraid to play with the word combinations a bit.

When you set up your gig pay close attention to what keywords your competition is using.

Look at their title and the gig description – do you see the keywords?

Think about your buyer as you write your description. What does he/she need and want from you?

What keywords come to mind?

If you are hitting your head against the wall- use the Google Keyword Tool aka Planner to generate ideas. Type the words generated into Fiverr one by one and see what comes up in the search.

Here is a link to the tool https://adwords.google.com/keywordtool

Don't be afraid to make some choices and get your gigs set up.

You can (and probably will) make changes to your keywords.

Later we will discuss looking at your gig analytics to see how your gigs are performing.

Ad Copy

I am going to be very, very blunt here – there are many people who offer many things on Fiverr.

The one complaint I see the most are about people who claim to be based in the USA and then their grammar (or lack of) and writing ability (or lack of) shows something is amiss.

If you are going to offer a gig that requires any type of writing or communication skills you want to let potential buyers know you are capable of delivering what may be needed.

I often include the words USA educated and USA based in my descriptions. I think this has helped my conversion rate considerably.

If you are a reader from outside the USA, please ensure your comprehension of English language (including slang) is up to par. This is being stated to help you, not insult you in any way.

As a buyer on Fiverr, I've worked with numerous Fiverr freelancers.

Many freelancers are outside the USA. My top Pinterest freelancer is outside the States yet I've used his service more times than I can recall and I've referred others to him. His communication skills are top level.

I had to interview numerous Fiverr freelancers offering the same service that he does before I found him.

You'll meet a lot of awesome buyers on Fiverr.

Many are professionals needing help with SEO, copy, proofing, web design etc.

Many potential buyers will interview freelance candidates before selecting one.

Communication is the key. Making sure your gig is properly described is crucial.

If you aren't 100% confident about your description and worry that your spelling or word use may be incorrect- hire a proofreader on Fiverr to review your gig description. It will be well worth the $5 you spend.

Adding Tags

Right under the description you'll see a place for tags. You need a minimum of 3 tags

Tags are keywords.

What words will your buyers be using when they look for gigs like yours?

Once again, I also look at my competition and see what keywords that they are using.

I test and measure these tags. If I set up a gig and it isn't performing I add tags and /or the description.

As with your other copy, you can add more tags later so don't become frazzled – just select some tags using pertinent keywords and get the gig up.

Keep in mind – we are ADDING tags not removing tags.

Why? Because people may save your gig for future reference and then purchase. If they happened to choose it due to selecting a certain tag and you REMOVE the tag it will no longer be in their saved searches.

Additional Comments Regarding Creating Your Gig Copy

As mentioned, I find it very valuable to look at other sellers' gigs that are similar to mine. I review their description and their keywords.

Then I look at their reviews – what stands out most?

If anything negative is posted – what is it?

Then I craft my ad.

The one thing I'm not too fond of is that Fiverr appears to have a very tight limit regarding how many times one can use a word in a description.

You have quite a bit of room regarding content but it often is a bit more difficult as for example if you were offering SEO, the word SEO in your gig description is highly limited.

I use synonyms often – just look the word up online and see what synonyms that you have available.

Also- please keep in mind every time you tweak your gig copy – in any way- there may be a delay in the gig going live as the Fiverr staff will review it.

Sometimes the delay is just minutes but I've heard of delays over a day occurring.

I prefer to test and measure my ad copy. If you choose to duplicate the steps I've followed, you will need to decide if you wish to go down the same path that I did or not.

Images

I have a collection of royalty free images from other projects.

I bought the images from Dreamstime.com.

You may have photos you've taken or other sources for images but if not, Dreamstime.com is a good starting point.

You buy credits and then use the credits to buy images. You download the images and then resize them as needed to fit on Fiverr.

If you use Dreamstime.com you can buy the smaller images – I use the ones labeled as 0. They cost very little and can be re-used as needed.

I recently saw another seller using images that it looked like she created using PowerPoint. I may experiment with the same idea in the future as the images were eye catching.

When I first started on Fiverr, I used random eye-catching images that I already had which saved a start -up cost for images.

However, recently Fiverr flagged a couple of mine and asked that I change the image to ones that fit the gig.

So for example, if you are doing a gig such as likes on Facebook – you are better off with an image of a person on a computer or royalty free Facebook image not one of a bumble bee.

I test and measure response for each gig. I occasionally change the image shown for a gig to see if the conversions change.

Great Examples of Excellent Copy & Images

This Fiverr seller offers a resume service

http://fiverr.com/alb8475/make-your-resume-awesome-to-land-you-the-job-you-want

The photo caught my attention. It obviously has done the same for others as this gig is producing sales and great reviews.

http://fiverr.com/radishcat/crochet-a-beard-for-you

This one I am including as the image really pops. His description is good and as he states he is offshore, I can live with the typos that I noticed in his copy. His copy overall though clearly spells out the offer.

http://fiverr.com/drawyourphoto/draw-your-face-potrait-into-circle-logo

Unique gig idea (there are a few sellers with this idea and most seem to be doing well). Her copy is good. Take a look at her tags – plentiful and relevant.

http://fiverr.com/rheazel/make-you-artwork-out-of-food

The image caught my attention immediately. The copy is good and the reviews add to her credibility.

http://fiverr.com/organic28/make-you-a-lovely-sterling-silver-multi-pearl-ring

This gig is for data entry. The offer is a good one and her photo was a smart choice for her image as she presents herself as a likable person in my opinion

http://fiverr.com/cmg236/enter-your-data-into-spreadsheet

It has been stated in numerous places online that Fiverr gigs with videos convert better.

I haven't done a video yet and have been pleased with my starting number of orders but -

I've read that having a video creates double the sales so we'll cover the topic in this book.

Being very blunt, I haven't seen any actual statistics to back the increased sales statement.

While it seems like a great conversion, I think one needs to test and measure to see how a video converts.

I may be doing a video in the future but don't let not having one hold you back from starting as you can achieve sales without one.

If you are going to do a video – some basic tips (using my infomercial production background)

Look at what is behind you on your video. If it is a bookshelf – is it dusty? Are there books and papers strewn about?

You don't have to be movie star good looking but you should be neatly dressed.

Think about what you are going to say.

Rehearse it – more than once.

Don't be afraid to scrap an idea and go a different route if the video doesn't turn out as planned or if you have a different idea.

I also suggest that if you do use a video clip – don't hesitate to test and measure a different creation of an idea comes to you regarding improving your video.

I will add – on a somewhat different note- I did book trailers (videos) for a few of my books and placed the videos on YouTube. I am seeing sales and that is the only promotion being done.

Many people are visual- they would rather watch a clip than read a paragraph. I definitely encourage you to test a video presentation on Fiverr.

These are a few examples of gigs with video clips that I think were done quite well.

I don't know these people and haven't utilized their services but as a marketer – I was impressed.

The first link is Robin. She is a proofreader. Note the background. Also note that she is neatly groomed, speaks slowly (important!) and has a very sincere way about her.

http://fiverr.com/robinoo/professionally-proofread-1000-words

This guy is from the U.K. I included him even though this isn't a video because he really comes across (in my opinion) as darn likable. I can see why he is getting the great flow of buyers and his signs aren't even professionally done – they are handwritten! But he did a great job in my opinion.

http://fiverr.com/oranjewebdesign/take-5-distinguished-photos-of-me-holding-a-fan-sign

This is Claire. I've come across her gigs a few times and although I haven't worked with her – I think you will immediately see why I selected her as an example. Stellar clip.
http://fiverr.com/silvervirtual/create-a-professional-quality-video-presentation-in-an-australian-accent

Note the background on this one – nice and clean- no clutter. She speaks well – I'd almost think she had a teleprompter in front of her but I think this is just the result of someone not rushing and perhaps re-doing the clip until she had it perfect. Great job in my opinion
http://fiverr.com/indica/tweet-your-message-and-guarantee-10-retweets?autoplay=true

This Canadian offers a detailed overview in very little time. Background is good. Color scheme is good.
Definitely makes the grade in my book as a video that is well done.
http://fiverr.com/kevinharwood/professionally-playtest-your-video-game

I liked this clip for a female voiceover as she provides numerous samples and also lists her credentials plus clear instructions.

http://fiverr.com/kym_voiceovers/deliver-a-professional-read-of-30-seconds-of-audio-to-you-for-voice-over-commercials-imaging-phonewebsite-narration-quick-turnaround

I like this video clip a lot. The seller makes origami stars. I've seen gigs offering origami do well on Fiverr and think this one may be held back by the 24 days needed to complete. Either way – some effort was put into this video

http://fiverr.com/lubeorigami/fold-a-special-message-in-an-origami-star

I liked this gig for numerous reasons. The seller gives a little tease of what he is offering in the clip. The gig is quite unusual and caught my attention. His presentation was clear and concise.

http://fiverr.com/magicdood/teach-you-3-business-card-easy-magic-tricks-great-for-networking

I wanted to show you a video or two for gigs offering writing a message on the sand. However the ones I found weren't ideal and bring up an important thing to remember- background noise.

I'm not going to post video links that I think aren't ideal as it isn't the purpose of this chapter to say someone's video isn't done well.

Obviously if you are offering a gig such as writing names/messages in the sand you will have the noise of the water that you'll need to work with so it doesn't drown out your presentation. Keep this in mind though and plan on doing the video when the wind is calm. Also add graphics so viewers can understand the message.

I then looked for a video writing a message using various things such as stones. The one I really liked had obvious misspellings in the description and with that being said, I didn't choose it as an example.

I hope the video clips I included help you to start thinking about videos that you could create for your Fiverr gigs.

Please keep in mind that sellers come and go on Fiverr. The links I've provided as examples may not work if a seller has moved on.

You can also do searches on Fiverr (and I suggest that you do) to find examples such as the ones I've shown you. I search on a regular basis so I can see what other sellers are doing, content, images etc.

Analytics and Useful Statistics

Fiverr has a section that shows all of your stats.

You'll be able to see how many people have looked at your gig and the conversions to sales plus other valuable information.

Be sure to check your stats and look at the Analytics. Also review the data shown for My Gigs as this is the activity generated by people looking at your gig and buying (or not).

This is how you will find this data:

Look on the main Fiverr page.

You'll see Sales at the top.

Click on Sales and under it in green font you'll see My Gig and also Analytics.

Analytics will give you a basic breakdown of orders and income.

My Gigs is where the meatier data is kept.

You'll find out how many impressions your gig has had in the last 30 days.

You'll also be able to see how many page views, how many clicks, how many sales and your conversion rate to sales.

I check the above data daily and encourage you to get in the habit of doing the same.

Revenue is listed right under My Gigs – this is helpful as you can see what income is pending and what income is ready for you to take.

Testing and Measuring for Optimum Success

The one common thread in marketing success is testing and measuring.

The measuring I am referring to keeping statistics and seeing what works, what doesn't work and knowing with certainty you are correct as you have data to prove it.

I have lost count of how many times I asked a client what was working and the conversation went something like this:

Client- We've found country music stations do the best.

Me – Please show me your stats to back this comment.

Dead silence.

Another one:

Client: Mary is our best media buyer. Hands down does the best job. Now Joe, he's a real problem and I'm thinking about firing him.

Me – Please show me your stats.

Client: Well – it's Obvious (this word is drawn out)

There are no stats to back the client's statement.

In the media buyer stats, I asked the client's IT department to pull the media history and I spent the evening in my hotel room reviewing the raw data.

The employee the client raved about was losing thousands and thousands of dollars weekly. She was rebooking (for weeks on end) media that didn't work – at all.

In five minutes time, I couldn't believe how poorly this employee was performing and she had been doing this for months.

Joe, on the other hand, while not a stellar media buyer, definitely wasn't at the bottom of the barrel.

On top of it, Mary was not negotiating her media at all. In one day I shaved $100,000 (yes you read that right) $100,000 off the price of the advertising that Mary had paid.

Now I think you'll see why keeping stats is so important to me and why I want to ensure you understand the importance of stats too.

The above examples aren't stated to make someone feel bad but so many times people think something is working and when we actually manage by statistics- we find that the client had an incorrect assumption.

We may also find that we had an incorrect assumption regarding a gig we are marketing or the value of the gig to our bottom line.

It takes about 14 days from the date you deliver on Fiverr until the funds are moved into an account that you can either take the revenue from or use the revenue to buy gigs.

With that being said, funds will come in in increments depending upon the flow of your orders.

You may see $4 one day and $24 the next.

You will need a PayPal account to send the funds to. Keep this in mind, you cannot change the PayPal account once you select it.

Also- if having a PayPal account is something new to you, I suggest you do not wait until sales start – set up the PayPal account right away.

You have to verify the account – PayPal removes tiny, tiny increments (as in a few cents) from your account and you will need to verify the exact amounts. It takes 2 to 3 business days to get this part done. When you sign up on PayPal this is all explained to you but now you have a heads up so you don't wait until the last minute to set up your PayPal account.

About 14 days after you deliver your gigs, the funds will be moved to Withdraw Your Revenues.

The PayPal button on Fiverr will change from grey to green and will become enabled.

The first time I moved money I found it rather confusing as I didn't know if it moved to PayPal.

I checked PayPal and could see it was processing.

I went back, refreshed the Fiverr page and then could see the funds were gone from the page 9as they were now in PayPal).

Fiverr also has something that they call a Fiverr Revenue Card. It is issue via MasterCard and is like a prepaid credit card.

MasterCard does charge a fee for the Fiverr Revenue Card.

I suggest that you use PayPal for payments if at all possible.

I think these sellers are on the very extreme end of what type of income one can generate from just one gig.

They also are hitting specific niches.

While the Average Joe may not see 3000 reviews for one gig – I wanted to include a few examples of the heavy hitters who are generating mega reviews from just one gig just so you see what is possible on Fiverr- it is pretty impressive.

This guy has over 3400 reviews and 100% rating!!!! He found a niche and has really built an income from it.

http://fiverr.com/aaliyaan/customize-wordpress-fix-wp-error-edit-themetemplate-or-css

Laura helps buyers with Facebook. Over 1500 votes thus far and keep in mind, many of her sales may be generating more income than just the basic $4.

http://fiverr.com/growwithlaura/help-you-with-marketing-and-engaging-your-fans-on-facebook

This gentleman has over 2000 reviews.   He's in France yet able to work with people all over the word regarding SEO

http://fiverr.com/markp/write-an-seo-action-plan-for-your-site-on-how-to-optimize-it-and-get-it-ranking

Putting Gigs on Hold

You are able to pause a gig by suspending it.

When would you do this? The reasons are numerous –

If you are traveling and not able to check for orders.

If you are ill.

If you have an abundance of orders (either from the gig you are pausing or from another one).

If you are selling a product (jewelry for example) and are running low on supplies.

If for some reason you can't deliver, suspending your gig is an option.

If you look at the page that shows "My Gigs" you'll see how you can suspend (or delete) gigs.

Fiverr Buy Requests- A Useful Resource & Revenue Stream

You'll find an area on Fiverr called Buyer Requests.

Depending upon your level you can reach out to a certain amount of buyers looking for specific gigs.

Working leads in this area has brought in a decent amount of sales for me.

The down side is – you are not allowed to write a personal message to the buyer.

If you click on their request, you have the option of choosing one of your available gigs to send to them as an option.

As the gigs selected from yours as options are for some reason often limited, sometimes the best choice of your gigs won't be an option for you to send,

This is a little quirky to me but I've managed to make do with it and think you should also be able to do so. I'm hoping Fiverr refines this process in the future.

So with this being said – if you check this area daily, you may be able to increase your buyers considerably depending on what is being requested and what you offer.

I have found the best time to check the Buyer Request area (and get an answer) is in the evenings. However this does vary and if possible try to check the Buyer Requests a few times each day.

Be realistic though – if you can't deliver what is being requested don't waste your time (or the buyer's time).

While on most days I will find several Buyer Requests to reply to there are days when I reply to zero.

Also, sometimes the buyer will not respond back to you or may respond weeks later.

In the long run, I think it is well worth it to work these leads daily.

Long Term and Bundled Gigs

Occasionally, I will come across a buyer via the Buyer Request section or through a buyer contacting me directly who wants a quote on a long term gig or a bundled gig.

As stated earlier, I'm not going to go into detail regarding the gigs that I offer as I don't want a reader to feel I am promoting myself as that is not the purpose of this book.

I will use the following as a generic example-

If I am offering social media posting services, the query might be for a quote to do the gig daily for a month.

Another one asked if he gave me daily consistent business for a couple weeks would I do 3 posts versus 1 for each gig?

You need to decide if offers like these (or whatever a buyer suggests) work for you.

I just declined several last week as they wanted extensive research and time commitment and wanted to pay very little- one wanted 45 posts (usually would be 45 x$4 per gig for) He wanted to pay less than a $1 each.

This would equal 8 or 9 gigs but I would be doing 5 times the work for each one.

In this case I declined as he wanted me to also do a lot of research (on his behalf) and there was zero guidance regarding what was wanted even after I attempted to get clarification 3 times.

In a previous mentioned above I did 3 posts for the price of one. However, the posts were not lengthy and the buyer had clear directions. We worked together well.

Communicating

It is important to communicate with your buyer.

When the person buys your gig they'll receive an auto-responder message from Fiverr.

You will have written this message when you set up your gig.

I always thank the seller for their order and then list what info that I need to get started.

I then follow up and let them know I am working on the order or will be soon.

Often throughout the order process I send a brief message especially if the order isn't delivered for a couple days.

Communicating helps to get good reviews and repeat business.

It is also just treating others like you would like to be treated if you were the buyer.

Some of my gigs take up to 4 days to finish.

While I am pushing to finish earlier, I still reach out beforehand and update the buyer.

I may write something such as – Hi, I'm just checking in to let you know I've been working on your project.

Buyers appreciate the updates and numerous times buyers have mentioned my excellent communication in their review of my gig.

Over Deliver

Over Delivering means going above and beyond what is requested or expected.

Over Delivering has been a key piece in my success on Fiverr. It fits in well with communicating too.

However, I also write my gigs with over delivering in mind.

A few examples:

If I know in most cases a gig that takes 2 minutes is one I can usually get to in one day, I may market it as taking 4 days and then I deliver it "early".

I also have extra "bonuses" that I may add on such as if I am posting to my LinkedIn contacts one time, I may post two days as a bonus versus just the one day.

I may offer suggestions to buyers or point out typos or formatting issues.

People appreciate it a lot when they see that you are willing to go the extra mile.

Declining Requests

We just talked about Over Delivering but what if someone wants you to do something simply not feasible? Or if it is something that makes you uncomfortable?

I've had a few situations when this occurred.

Just to give you some examples – someone wanted several product reviews for the price of one.

In some cases, I may over deliver and do three reviews for the price of one if I know the seller wants more reviews.

Or if the reviews requested are just a few words.

We discussed this scenario earlier when we discussed bundled gigs.

I know how long I am to spend on each gig – as we calculated this earlier, remember?

So if I know the gig takes me two minutes, I would need a very good reason to accept a request for the gig that changes the parameters of the gig and takes 20 minutes or even worse, a day.

Another one – and this is common – wanted me to do a review NOW – as in the next 30 minutes and didn't want to pay the rush charge.

If I didn't have any gigs on deck and this request came in, then yes, I'd probably do it but if I am up against a time crunch especially if it involves clients who paid a rush fee, I would decline the gig.

You are not desperate for business – keep this in mind. Desperation will show through and even if you are waiting to finally get your first gig, if someone sends a request that just isn't right you can pass on it.

Don't accept a request to do a gig that is not something you normally do. You want to deliver and deliver well not be winging it with a project you've never done before.

If you are doing reviews of websites and someone wants you to test and review a phone app- you can decline to work with them.

I've had a few other requests that I won't go into detail regarding but basically the potential buyers wanted me to do something I considered unethical regarding a product review. In all the cases, I politely declined the offer to work with them.

Cancels

I recently contacted Fiverr Support as I have formally requested that they find a way to deal with Cancels that are simply not the fault of the freelancer (seller).

I currently have 3 cancels – 1 is because someone hit the order button twice.

 Number 2 was because the buyer did not send the information   needed despite numerous requests from me.

He then claimed he had sent it and the problem was on my end. I had plenty of other orders coming through for the exact same gig at the same time so the challenge was not on this end.

Number 3 was because a buyer bought a gig and asked me to do something not offered in the gig and not something I was even capable of doing.

I am hoping Fiverr does come up with a way to monitor and remove from our stats any cancellations like the ones above that are created through no fault of the freelancer.

Fiverr is growing in leaps and bounds and despite this, they are always beyond fast (and helpful) in responding to my queries.

You are able to find a lot of info in the Help Forums and I suggest you look there first but if you need help beyond the forum, Customer Support is an option.

You Can Lead a Horse to Water

You've probably heard the saying that you can lead a horse to water but you can't make 'em drink.

Depending on your Fiverr gig offering, this may become a mantra you will be repeating more than a few times.

One of my gigs offers marketing advice. In most cases the buyer will respond and send information that I request from them.

In most cases they will implement the changes that I make or at least indicate that they will be implementing them.

Occasionally though I have a buyer who just doesn't do what I suggest. This is not an uncommon occurrence as when I have done consulting (often with large publicly traded companies) I would sometimes encounter the same situation.

I offer advice, the client doesn't implement and then grouses that they didn't see results, or didn't learn anything etc.

This same sort of buyer does crop up on Fiverr. I urge you to keep notes on projects and keep the emotion out of the situation. If a buyer grouses a bit, kindly re-iterate what you've asked them and what info that you still need them to provide.

For example – I reviewed a commercial for a client and made numerous comments regarding changes that really needed to be made.

The client was very slow in following up with me. Remember you are on a time line and you need to have the gig wrapped up and delivered in a specified amount of time.

So in this case, the client had not finished (actually he didn't even start what was advised). My part was done as I had offered the advice.

Going the extra mile, as we want to over deliver as discussed earlier, I let him know that once the commercial was revised I'd look at it – no additional charge.

I also nicely reminded him that the ball was in his court as he needed to revise his commercial, there was nothing more that I could do.

While he left a positive review, he added comments implying he expected more and not stating that he hadn't supplied what was needed or that I had gone the extra mile and helped him with things that were not part of the gig.

I could have stewed a bit or replied with a snotty comment but I didn't.

The main thing is – don't allow someone's attitude to get to you. You've delivered what was requested and hopefully delivered earlier than planned.

Reviews

I've read complaints from sellers in the Fiverr forums regarding buyers who don't leave reviews.

I'm sorry but not leaving reviews is common. Most likely you will have clients who do not leave reviews or maybe months later will suddenly do the review.

I received a positive review today from a seller that I worked with over two months ago.

I always thank the buyer for working with me.

My first goal is to build solid and sincere rapport with the buyer. Then deliver what is needed and wanted by the buyer –over delivering if at all possible.

I've mentioned in the message that the buyer receives when ordering a gig that great reviews are my goal but in testing having the message or not – I don't see that mentioning it makes too much difference.

I've seen sellers almost hound buyers to leave good reviews and I just don't think it is the right way to operate.

If the buyer doesn't leave a review, I don't think twice about it. My thoughts are on what I can offer to increase my buyers not worry about one person who didn't leave a review.

Tip Jar Gigs

There are sellers who add a "tip jar" gig. In other words the buyer can buy the tip gig to tip the seller.

I do not have a tip gig as I focus on creating gigs that bring in traffic and convert to sales,

Having a tip jar gig is a decision you will need to make.

However, keep in mind you can only offer up to 20 gigs (as a Level 2 seller) and you want your gigs to be revenue producing options.

Less is More- or is it?

When I first started on Fiverr, I read over and over the same two topics.

The first one being make your gig description short and sweet and the second one – you may find this as interesting as I did – limit the amount of gigs you offer (you can have up to 20) and keep them associated with each other.

Don't be a Jack of All Trades was something I read more than a few times.

I made my gig description for one gig longer than the others. Sales started immediately

Thus debunking the myth of shorter is better. I then tested the description – shortening and lengthening. The longer version converted better.

By longer – I am not writing several lines but more than a word or two.

Then we have the amount of gigs – I have created as many as I'm allowed which I think is 20 at this time.

I paused (suspended) several gigs to see if less is more.

Please note I paused gigs that were low producers and newer ones who were still in the testing phase.

The orders for my well producing gigs skidded to a halt.

I restarted all my gigs and the orders (for the gigs that hadn't been suspended) increased.

Perhaps this was a fluke but this is why I will say over and over- test and measure.

Don't buy into something as being a "rule" just because you've read it- test and measure for yourself.

Upsells

I've read more than a few times that where one starts making money on Fiverr is when you can offer upsells.

Upsells are things such as Rush for an extra $5, $10 or $20.

Or Double the amount of Tweets (or whatever) for an extra $5, $10 or 420.

In my situation, adding Rush hasn't increased my orders much at all.

Depending on what gigs you offer- Rush or extra add ons may skyrocket your income.

The key is- test and measure.

Fiverr Forums

Fiverr has a very extensive forum for both buyers and sellers. Sellers are encouraged to participate and help others.

I will dig around the forums for insight as well as updates.

http://forum.fiverr.com/

I've read that Fiverr keeps tabs on Seller participation and that participation may help you reach a higher ranking in the Fiverr searches (when someone types in keywords looking for specific gigs).

I do encourage you to use the forums as they contain a wealth of information.

However, realize that buyers and sellers alike utilize the forums.

Often a seller does become a buyer and vice versa.

With that being said, don't fall prey to having a meltdown in the Ranting Pot forum or any other place on the forums where people are complaining about buyers.

Being negative won't win you any friends (or sales) and if a potential buyer sees you've written a scathing post about someone not tipping, not giving a review or whatever – it lowers your attractiveness as a vendor.

Also – there are things that all the ranting in the world won't change such as people not "tipping" and people not giving reviews.

Instead of spending your time complaining, send that time studying your analytics, tweaking a gig or marketing.

Focus on revenue generating activities not dead ends.

You can create your gigs and just wait for people to find you.

You may get a few sales right out of the gate depending on your gig offerings.

You can amplify your possible sales though by doing some basic marketing.

You're sitting on the gold mine of marketing opportunities as you can utilize other freelancers' services to market your gigs.

There are plenty (and that's an understatement) of people offering to market your service to people on Twitter, Facebook, Pinterest, Linked In and other social media outlets.

This is an area where you do need to ask about what you're buying.

Someone offering to tweet your message to 1 million people is not a good choice if the 1 million people are cat lovers in Brazil and you are selling SEO services.

On the other hand, if you are selling jewelry, someone pinning your images on Pinterest for $5 is worth a look.

Don't be afraid to ask questions of other sellers regarding the demo (demographics) of people that they will market your offer to.

With my book marketing, Twitter has been my weakest marketing vehicle. It doesn't do badly but Pinterest has been a very strong marketing tool.

Yet the other day, I did a little Twitter marketing, Bing/Yahoo paid search marketing and Google AdWords marketing.

I received a query from a person who stated she saw my Twitter post. The Google AdWords had zero clicks and the Bing/Yahoo fared better but still was beat out by the Twitter buy.

Keep stats (statistics) on your marketing so you know what source worked and what creative (what ad) worked and also what didn't work.

So what should you choose to do as a Seller? Maybe you already have some ideas.

Maybe you do SEO now.

Maybe you already are doing voiceovers for commercials and that's what you'd like to offer.

Maybe you're a wizard at Facebook banners or YouTube banners.

But what else could you do if you aren't an SEO (search engine optimization) pro?

Below are several gig ideas. I've also included linked to sellers offering the gigs so you have examples. As sellers come and go, you may find a link is no longer active.

If so, you can just do a search on Fiverr for puppets, SEO, proofreading etc.

SEO

Proofreading

Translation

Puppets

Website Review

Product Review

Book Promo (I've used this seller's services numerous times and he always hits the ball out of the park)

Writing name in sand on beach (you can write names/messages on about anything and with the right presentation and marketing, you'll see sales)

Video Testimonials

Making ornaments

Writing names on items

What else can you think of?

By now you may be wondering what exactly you should consider doing on Fiverr.

Based on my own experience – I will tell you that there is no right or wrong answer.

Choose something – the main thing is getting started. You may find you need to tweak your gig or that it gets buyers immediately or none at all.

You may find (as I did) that a gig that you thought was THE one – did nothing.

Or one gig received a ton of traffic but no buyers.

Or one gig consistently produces sales each week.

What I did was test and measure and not be afraid to fail or full a gig.

I looked at what I could offer people – no matter how simple.

Review a website.

Review a diet product.

Proofreading.

Send out a message to my Twitter followers.

Send out a message to my Linked In followers.

If I was good at crafting things, there are plenty of things I would test.

There's a woman who spells out messages with alphabet spaghetti.

Another gig offers names or a message written on Christmas ornaments – you don't get the actual ornaments. You receive a photo of her creation (emailed to you).

The main thing is- jump in. Get started.

Create your gigs and decide how you're going to market yourself.

Still stumped?

Email me at loerapublishing@hotmail.com and tell me what you're thinking about offering as a gig. I'll help you brainstorm a bit.

Beyond Fiverr

Gigs you test on Fiverr may end up becoming full time freelance projects for you on your own.

Fiverr is a great place to test the water for various services.

It gives you the opportunity to have thousands of people searching through the Fiverr site for various gigs and you are not spending a dime for advertising, do not have the expense of a website, merchant account etc.

Let's say for example – you test 20   gigs.   One of them, proofreading, really brings in the business on Fiverr.

You hone your skills and delivery time.

You decide to expand a bit and do some marketing (using fellow Fiverr freelancers).

You then decide to build a basic website (GoDaddy or WordPress) and start your own freelance proofreading business.

You'll still have your Fiverr business and NEVER EVER try to move Fiverr buyers over to your personal freelance site.

You can have the best of both worlds – your Fiverr gigs and your own growing freelance business.

Your Fiverr gigs will teach you how to deliver on time, what people are looking for and also they can be a great revenue source for you.

.You can look at your sales and see how much you've made total and also see monies pending (it takes 14 days after you complete a gig for the money to come into your account).

Being a freelancer on your own requires more discipline and also more marketing (even if you use Fiverr freelancers for marketing help).

What is good about Fiverr is you can generate a steady income and you also quickly find out how much potential your idea has once you've created the gig.

Social Media can play a big part in helping you promote.

You can utilize other freelancers on Fiverr to promote for you.

You can also use your earned money from Fiverr to pay for freelancers which is a nice perk and makes buying services easier.

Ways to market include Facebook, LinkedIn, Twitter and Pinterest.

Pinterest is growing in leaps and bounds.

If you 're offering something such as writing names/messages in sand or making origami- Pinterest should be Stop Number One on your marketing list.

If you're new to Pinterest or don't have time to add pins, there are Fiverr freelance options available.

The main thing is that you need to get your name and gig out in front of as many people as possible.

You need to establish a platform of what works for your specific gig and what doesn't.

You may find one gig receives the most leads via Pinterest marketing and another gig's sales increase when Pinterest marketing is implemented.

While each gig is totally different – in my case Bing/Yahoo paid ads and Google paid ads did zero for my business.

I test and measure all marketing. One test was Google against Bing/Yahoo. I had read numerous articles about Bing and how it is out performing Google.

I'll say this – my cost per click was way less and I had much more traffic (I tested the exact same ad – you need to do this to have an accurate test).

So when I saw neither of these were producing after a few days (less than a week) but were costing money – I added a Fiverr gig.

The Fiverr gig – it was to promote to Twitter followers – produced 5 sales the first day. Some of the sales had upsells (Rush or additional services) so my $5 investment paid off well.

I promptly cancelled the Bing and Google paid ads.

This example should show you the importance of testing and measuring your marketing.

Do not beat a dead horse – I could have continued with Google and Bing (as an example) but why? I was not making any revenue - they were costing me money.

Once you're established – you may want to do longer tests but I've found cash flow wise and also based on my experience – you need to see at least one sale in the first few days or it is time to move on to another test.

My addition of the Fiverr buy proved instantly that it was not my ad copy. I used the same copy for all three tests.

In your case- Google and/or Bing may produce a ton of business. In my case neither one performed.

This is why testing and measuring is so important. Don't just blindly throw money into marketing – you need to work methodically and monitor your results.

Keep in mind, I didn't randomly choose a Twitter gig. I asked several sellers and did a Buyers Request to narrow down possible candidates. I've since used this seller's gig three times and plan on continuing as it drives traffic and orders.

If the idea of marketing still leaves you in a tail spin – contact me at loerapublishing@hotmail.com I'll offer you some pointers and make suggestions regarding what I would do marketing-wise.

If you understand the idea of marketing yet do not have the time – I would be happy to introduce you to freelancers who can help you market your gigs. Just email me at the above address and explain your situation.

Wrap Up

Thank you for taking the time to read my book. If you are thinking about becoming a seller on Fiverr- get started now. You could be sitting on a money making gig.

If you have gigs listed on Fiverr and are not getting sales, I hope this book offered some insight.

If you still need help-my offer stands. Email me and tell me about your favorite gig and perhaps I can give you some additional marketing tips.

Sincerely,

Diana